STAGE FRIGHT
AND
WHAT TO DO ABOUT IT

STAGE FRIGHT

AND

WHAT TO DO ABOUT IT

BY

DWIGHT EVERETT WATKINS, A. M.
Associate Professor of Public Speaking
University of California, Berkeley

Author of *An Introduction to the Art of Speech, Effective Speech, The Convincing Word, Etc.*

AND

HARRISON M. KARR, Ph. D.
Instructor in Public Speaking
University of California, Los Angeles

Author of *Your Speaking Voice*

Illustrations by
ZADIE HARVEY

EXPRESSION COMPANY — PUBLISHERS
BOSTON - - - - MASSACHUSETTS

TREATMENT

STAGE FRIGHT
AND
WHAT TO DO ABOUT IT

TREATMENT I

THE SYMPTOMS OF STAGE FRIGHT

Doubtless, at some time in your life, you've had an attack of stage fright.

Otherwise, you wouldn't be reading this little book.

But here's a comforting thought.

You probably never had a complete attack! That is, you probably never had all the distressing symptoms at once!

You were uncomfortable enough, to be sure!

But some people, in an attack of stage fright, are uncomfortable in one way, and others in another.

One of the most common ways in which stage fright manifests itself is in *trembling*. Most people in describing their stage fright mention this symptom first. They say: "Why, I just trembled all over!"

Trembling Knees

Some people seem to feel this trembling most in their knees. Their knees seem to "knock together." They sometimes stop the "knocking together" by placing the weight all on one leg. But, then, the other knee trembles worse than before! One speaker in describing how his knees acted said: "If my hips had emulated my knees, I would have been ejected from the hall for indulging in that kind of a dance!"

Others feel the trembling in their hands. If they are giving a public address when the attack comes on, and if they are using notes, the notes tremble so much that they can scarcely read them. And not using notes seems to help these people not a bit. The hands go right on trembling just the same — only now they tremble in their pockets or behind their backs!

Trembling Hands

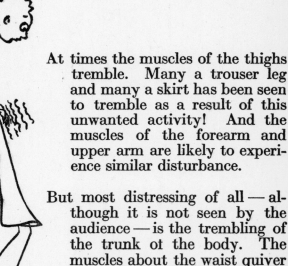

At times the muscles of the thighs tremble. Many a trouser leg and many a skirt has been seen to tremble as a result of this unwanted activity! And the muscles of the forearm and upper arm are likely to experience similar disturbance.

But most distressing of all — although it is not seen by the audience — is the trembling of the trunk of the body. The muscles about the waist quiver like a hairless Mexican dog in a Colorado blizzard!

"Oh, This Internal Earthquake!"

And the trembling inside the body is even worse! There are rumblings and shakings that make the victim feel that he is staging an internal earthquake that will never die down!

"Will Somebody Please Put Salt on This Bird's Tail?"

Meanwhile, how the *heart pounds!* People who in ordinary life "have never had a heart," feel as if some giant bird were imprisoned in their chests and as if that bird were beating its life out against the bars of their ribs!

The pulses, too, hammer at the temples, and at the throat. A 16½ collar feels as if it were only a 13½! Women feel their pulses jumping in their ears like so many leaping frogs entered in a Mark Twain race up and down their eustachian tubes!

"And how I blushed!" "Was my face red!" The *rush of blood* to the neck, the ears, the face, feels like a spray of warm water suddenly let loose over the skin. And, knowing that the blush is fiery red, and that the audience is probably aware of it, the fright-stricken victim feels more uncomfortable than ever. Sometimes he becomes even purple, and people in the audience fear for his blood pressure.

The *breath*, too, *is disturbed.* There is a tendency to pant. It seems there is not enough air in the whole world to fill the lungs! If the victim is speaking, he feels he must keep going.

The words must be got out somehow. And the more he struggles, and the more he tries to finish his sentences before *all* his breath is gone, the worse condition he finds himself. Each pause for breath seems like a million years! Consequently, he never gets a full breath and goes from bad to worse.

"How pale you got!" says a friend to the speaker, actor, or singer, when he comes off the platform or stage. Yes, he probably did *get pale* — pale between his blushes! And he says he felt cold. Of course he was cold when he became pale! Who doesn't feel cold when he becomes "pale as a sheet!"

Maybe the victim says *"the cold shivers" ran up and down his spine.* This, too, is a symptom. It goes with the pallor. One moment there is a flash of heat, when the blush comes on, and the next there is a chill as the paleness sets in.

" Now, Bring on That Audience!"

Along with the chill, also, the victim of stage
fright is likely to say that the *hair on the
back of his head and neck stood up.* Very
likely it did. And he may have had "goose-
flesh," too.

"Whenever I speak," John Dryden once said, "a *cold sweat* trickles down all over my limbs as if I were dissolving in water!" John Dryden was not the first to experience such a state. Nor was he the last. Many a singer, actor, or speaker has felt that same cold clamminess. But it is not always a cold sweat! Sometimes it is a tepid flood. The victim wipes his forehead with his handkerchief, wipes his hands, and really perspires as if he were chopping wood.

If the victim of stage fright has eaten a hearty meal just before his performance, often it happens that his *stomach feels as if it were filled with lead*. Sometimes there is a

Get the Mops!

feeling of inward churning. So severe is this
disturbance of digestion at times that a
violent fit of nausea ensues as soon as the
victim is off the platform.

The *salivary glands*, too, *often refuse to function.*
The mouth becomes absolutely dry. Very
literally, "the tongue cleaves to the roof of
the mouth." There must be swallowing after
each word in an effort to start the mouth
secretions.

If stage fright were really confined to the symptoms already described, it might not be
dreaded quite so much. For such symptoms
might escape the attention of the audience.
But, sad to say, the effects of stage fright are
much more devastating. They often affect
the speaking, singing, or acting so much that
the stage fright becomes very distressing to
the audience as well as the performer.

There is often much fidgeting. The victim
shuffles his feet, constantly changes his position, plays with his watch chain, toys with
his pencil, buttons and unbuttons his coat,
puts his hands in his pockets and then takes
them out again, plays leapfrog with the
knife and fork at the banquet table, rolls and
unrolls, or folds and unfolds his notes or his
napkin. He leans on the table or desk, or
sways back and forth. Sometimes he resorts
to drinking glass after glass of water, in his
attempt to moisten his mouth and throat.

Once in the House of Representatives, when a speaker tried to overcome his fright by thus drinking water, at the same time voci-

Running a Windmill with Water

ferously ranting, a wag arose to a point of order and inquired of the Speaker whether it was in accord with the rules of the House **"for a windmill thus to be run with water!"**

If Only He Were in Congress, He Might Collect Mileage for this Speech!

At another time, when one of the members of the House kept walking up and down the aisle as he spoke, it was inquired whether the member intended "to collect mileage for his speech!"

Women often bite their fingernails or their lips. Some play with a belt buckle or a strand of fringe. Many turn Lady Macbeth and wring their hands.

Never does the voice behave as it should. It trembles. Initial parts of sentences are repeated. Stammering sets in. Often words are transposed. One fright-stricken victim began his speech by saying, "It is with great pleasure that tonight I rise to speak to my feet!" Another said in the heat of rapid utterance, "That shows to go you!"

The pitch of the voice rises and rises. Sometimes the tone thins out until it can scarcely be heard. In extreme cases there is no voice at all! With certain people the voice becomes breathy and husky. With others, there is a nervous clearing of the throat. Some repeat *er*, or *eh*, or *ah*, or some other vocal syllable between almost every two words.

Great rapidity of utterance often overtakes a speaker. He rushes along as if his life depended on getting through as quickly as possible. He slurs words, he mumbles.

The eyes, too, are affected. The performer stares at the ceiling or the floor. Sometimes he looks out of the window. But he never sees anything that he looks at! And he always tries to look anywhere but at the audience!

If a speaker or actor attempts to make gestures while under the influence of an attack of stage fright, the gestures are likely to be hurried, poorly timed — being a little too early or too late — or half finished. There are many scattered gestures, and gestures made close to the body. Sometimes the gestures degenerate into mere flips of the fingers. The elbow generally clings close to the side, and awkwardness and rigidity are plainly apparent.

The most distressing effect of stage fright, however, is probably the forgetting of the part. The singer forgets his notes or his words. The actor forgets his lines. The speaker forgets his next sentence or his next point. When this occurs, the attack of stage fright is at flood tide. The victim may have been able to cover up most of his other symptoms, but when a blank mind has overtaken him, he feels that the jig is up. He cannot stand there before the audience and just *do nothing*. He is up there to perform, and if he does not perform, he must acknowledge failure.

"Let Me See ... Where Was I?"

Of course, this torturing fear of failure only makes matters worse. The victim cannot think what he is to do next because he is too busy thinking about his own silence and what the audience will think if he fails. So the pause becomes longer and longer—it may be only a few seconds in duration according to actual time, but to the victim it seems ages! And thus a vicious spiral is set up — the longer the pause, the greater the fear, and the greater the fear, the longer the pause, until at last utter panic ensues. At times, the artist has to frankly admit the state he is in and leave the platform or sit down. Once a member of the British Parliament who, when attempting to give his maiden speech, was forced to sit down even before he had uttered his first sentence, aroused the question by one of the older members of Parliament as to whether or not the speaker had really "lost his virginity!"

"Wow! This Collar Is Tight!"

The exact opposite of forgetting what is to be said often attacks a speaker. So many thoughts come flooding to his mind that he cannot pick out any particular one for utterance. But the effect is just the same — a complete silence.

Inexperienced actors, singers, and speakers are not the only ones attacked by stage fright. Even the most experienced, the most famous, the most talented suffer attacks at times.

George Washington, in his first inaugural, was so "visibly perturbed that his hand trembled and his voice shook so that he could scarcely be understood."

Eva Le Gallienne, when asked, after her one thousandth performance, whether or not she had experienced stage fright, said: "Yes. And it gets worse every year!"

Boris Karloff told an interviewer: "I shudder and shake before every scene — after twenty-five years, too!"

John B. Gough, the famous temperance lecturer of the last century, had such an attack of stage fright on one occasion that he could not think how to start his lecture, and finally began: "Ladies and Gentlemen, I have nothing to say. It is not my fault that I am here!"

Madame Schumann-Heink once said: "I grow so nervous before a performance, I become sick, almost. I want to go home!"

Maurice Chevalier says of his stage fright: "While I stand in the wings waiting to go on, my knees knock together and I dry the perspiration from my hands, then from my forehead, and then from my hands again.

"*. . . And Nothing Came Out!*"

Always before I go on I am frightened. At
first it was so, now it is so, and I think it
will always be so. Yes, when I am an old
man I will pull my long white beard and
tremble in fear that tonight they will not like
Grandfather Chevalier."

Ernesto Brúmen is authority for the statement
that the great pianist Rubenstein would
pace nervously up and down before a concert, and was extremely nervous during the
opening number.

It is said that Nathaniel Hawthorne was
drenched in cold perspiration at the thought
of speaking at a public dinner.

A recently developed form of stage fright is
found in what is known as "mike fever,"
which attacks speakers before the microphone in broadcasting stations. This form
does not differ from the common forms. The
same symptoms are present. Charlie Chap-
lin had a bad case of it the first time he attempted a broadcast. He paced the floor,
muttering over and over, "Twenty million
people, twenty million people!" He rehearsed his opening joke several times and
when the time came for him to deliver it he
almost had a spasm.

It is said that Joan Crawford, in order to steady herself before the microphone, kicks off her shoes and stands in her stocking feet while broadcasting. Further, she has a chair in the studio screwed to the floor, so she can have something solid against which to lean.

"BUCK FEVER"

"Mike Fever"

But artists, such as actors, singers, and public speakers, are not the only ones to be attacked by stage fright. Prize fighters, sprinters, baseball players, football players, billiard players, lovers, and those seeking employment are equally subject to it.

Hank Greenberg, the first baseman for the Detroit Tigers in 1935, gave out the following interview just before the beginning of the world series that year. Said he: "What's the use of trying to be so sophisticated about the series? The thought of playing before all those people, and for all that money, gets me plenty excited. Listen! Last year I was so nervous before the series started that I couldn't eat!"

"Now, If Only I Can Catch It Between Jiggles!"

If you take a raw young boy from the country, where he has been used to a checkered red and white table-cloth, steel knives and forks with wooden handles, and heavy earthenware dishes, and seat him at a brilliantly appointed city banquet table, set with sparkling crystal, dainty china, and shining silver, with beautiful women, beautifully gowned, all about him, he will be very lucky if he doesn't upset the jelly in his lap before the evening is over!

The conventional stage attitude of an out-of-work employe seeking a job is one of shiftiness and nervousness. The applicant shuffles his feet, mumbles his words, and twists his hat in his hands.

Lovers Often Have It Worse than Speakers!

When the lover pulls the bouquet from under his coat, pushes the doorbell button, and waits for the appearance of his newest sweetheart, his heart pounds just as much as that of the young speaker beginning his first speech.

But in spite of all the tortures of stage fright, it is generally admitted that, usually, after the first few minutes of a performance the feeling wears away.

On the very occasion when John B. Gough experienced the attack of stage fright which caused him to begin with the words, "Ladies and Gentlemen, I have nothing to say," he quickly recovered and spoke for an hour and a half with great power, moving his audience to laughter and tears.

Madame Schumann-Heink, although she said that before a performance she became so nervous that she was almost sick, followed up that statement by saying: "But after I have been on the stage for a few moments I am so happy, nobody can drag me off!"

Madame Schumann-Heink

TREATMENT II

THE CAUSES OF STAGE FRIGHT

Do you wish to get rid of stage fright?

Then you ought to know its causes.

Only by knowing the causes of stage fright, can you hope to remove them, and thus get rid of your fear.

But to understand thoroughly the causes back of stage fright, you ought to know something about the emotions in general.

Now, the human nervous system is made up of two great divisions.

They are:

1. The central nervous system and
2. The autonomic nervous system.

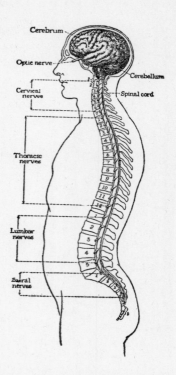

General View of the Central Nervous System

Reprinted from *The Human Body* by Logan Clendening, M. D., by permission
of and special arrangement with Alfred A. Knopf, Inc., authorized publishers

The central nervous system is composed of the
   brain, the spinal cord, and the various
   branches of the spinal cord.

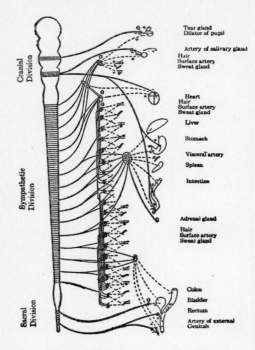

Tear gland
Dilator of pupil

Artery of salivary gland
Hair
Surface artery
Sweat gland

Heart
Hair
Surface artery
Sweat gland

Liver

Stomach

Visceral artery

Spleen

Intestine

Adrenal gland

Hair
Surface artery
Sweat gland

Colon

Bladder

Rectum

Artery of external
Genitals

Cranial Division

Sympathetic Division

Sacral Division

The Autonomic Nervous System

From *Bodily Changes in Pain, Hunger, and Rage*, W. B. Cannon; D. Appleton-Century Co., N. Y.

The autonomic nervous system has three divisions:

　　1. The cranial (head) division, which is connected with the upper part of the spinal cord and the brain.

2. The sacral (pelvic) division, which is connected with the lower part of the spinal cord.

3. The sympathetic division, which is connected with the middle part of the spinal cord.

Now, all the internal organs — the heart, lungs, stomach, liver, intestines, kidneys, etc. — are connected with the sympathetic (middle) division of the autonomic system and *either* with the cranial (head) division *or* the sacral (pelvic) division.

Likewise, the ductless (endocrine) glands — the thyroid, adrenal, pituitary, etc. — are similarly connected.

Further, the smooth (unstriped, involuntary) muscles near the surface of the body are connected exactly in the same way, that is, with the sympathetic (middle) division of the autonomic system and *either* with the cranial (head) division *or* the sacral (pelvic) division.

When the sympathetic (middle) division of the autonomic system is stimulated, it creates *one* sort of reaction, while the cranial (head) and the sacral (pelvic) divisions, when stimulated, produce a reaction *just opposite* in kind.

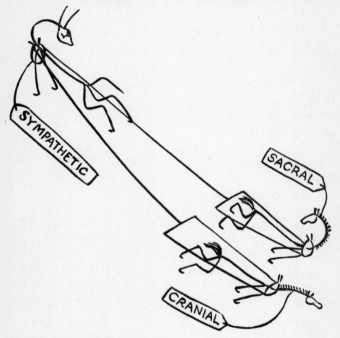

The Cranial and Sacral Divisions of the Autonomic Nervous System Work in Opposition to the Sympathetic Division

Thus, the sympathetic division and the cranial and sacral divisions work in opposition to each other and maintain a balance.

Impulses from the sympathetic division increase the activity of the heart, whereas impulses from the cranial division tend to slow it. Impulses from the sympathetic division also tend to decrease the glandular and muscular activities of digestion in both the upper and lower regions of the intestines, whereas impulses from the cranial division increase the activity of the upper regions, and impulses from the sacral division increase the activity of the lower regions.

The sympathetic division tends to work as a unit, while the cranial and sacral divisions may work separately.

Now, *ordinarily*, the autonomic system as a whole, that is, all three divisions — the sympathetic, the cranial, and the sacral — control the vital functions of the body without being influenced by the *central* nervous system to any great extent. But, *at times*, the central nervous system may send impulses into the autonomic system and affect its conduct. It is as if the central nervous system had delegated certain functions to the autonomic system, and trusts it implicitly to carry on all routine work connected with these functions, *but* had reserved to itself the *right to interfere* and issue orders *in cases of emergency*.

"This Is an Emergency! Give 'er All You've Got!"

Some of the impulses coming from the central nervous system may come as a result of *inherited pathways* (instinct) and some as a result of *pathways that have been built up by experience*, that is, *learned pathways*.

Thus, a noise in the dark, the perception of an enraged animal, an insult, may cause the central nervous system to send impulses into the autonomic system and influence its behavior.

"How I Can Run!"

Now, of course, there are sensory neurones (nerve cells) in all parts of the body, and, consequently, it is possible to become aware of the reactions that go on in the internal organs, the glands, and the unstriped muscles. This perception of the reactions of the internal organs, the glands, and the unstriped muscles (involuntary muscles) is called *feeling an emotion. Ordi-*

narily, we are not conscious of the activities of the body which are under the control of the autonomic system, but *when these activities become extraordinary*, we *do* feel them, and we are said to be *experiencing an emotion*.

STOMACH LIKE LEAD
KNEES TREMBLE
HAIR ON END
HANDS SHAKE

"*It's an Emergency all Right!*"

In fear (and stage fright, as its name implies, is a form of fear) the changes brought about by the impulses flowing from the central nervous system into the autonomic system are quite clearly marked.

In the first place, *all stomach movements tend to stop.* Further, *the glandular activities of digestion are cut down or stopped.* This means that the saliva ceases to flow, that the pancreatic and gastric juices are reduced in quantity.

The *reason* for these effects seems to lie in the turning of the bodily energy *away from* the digestive processes, thus allowing more bodily energy to flow into muscular activity.

Great changes in the circulation are also brought about. *The heart beats more rapidly and energetically.* The *arteries of the abdomen contract.* The *blood pressure rises.* The *respiratory muscles cause deeper and more frequent breathing.* The *sweat glands on the surface of the body are stirred into activity,* thus allowing more heat to escape from the body. The *tiny muscles about the roots of the hair of the body contract,* causing "goose-flesh" and a bristling of the hairs, such as is seen in a cat when he is frightened, and a tickling sensation or shiver.

The Adrenalin Twins

Along with these reactions, *the adrenal glands (two little glands just above the kidneys) discharge their fluid into the blood,* causing many more reactions. Thus, *adrenalin (the secretion of the adrenal glands) dimin-*

ishes further the glandular and muscular activities of digestion. It also *contracts further the abdominal arteries.* It *quickens and strengthens the action of the heart and respiratory muscles.* In the lungs, it *dilates the air passages*, thus allowing for the passage of more air, to carry off the waste products of the body. The adrenalin also affects the voluntary *muscles of the body, causing them to possess greater strength and endurance.* The liver, too, under the influence of the adrenalin, *pours into the blood greater amounts of its stored-up sugar, which is the fuel burned in muscular effort.* Further, *the liver discharges into the blood a substance which makes it clot more easily when exposed to the air, thus cutting down the possibility of bleeding to death in case of injury.*

It is plain that all these reactions are exactly those that would be called for in preparation for violent physical activity, *such as would be needed in FIGHT or FLIGHT.*

Call on Your Adrenals, Old Boy! You'll Need this Help, Whether You Fight or Run Away!

In other words, *these reactions were developed to aid self-preservation.*

But, now, *AS A CHECK upon all these activities set in motion by the sympathetic division of the autonomic system, there always exists the possibility of activity in the cranial and sacral divisions.*

"What a Beautiful Cranial and Sacral Evening!"

Under the stimulation of the cranial and sacral divisions of the autonomic system, the quiet processes of digestion are promoted. The flow of saliva is increased. The blood vessels of the abdomen are dilated. The general tone and activity of the intestines is improved. The heart is slowed down.

Such reactions arouse what have been called *the quiet and pleasurable* emotions. When we experience these emotions we have *a general sense of well-being.* Such a sense of well-being comes when we *hear beautiful music,* when we *enjoy our work,* when we are *engaged in agreeable conversation,* when we are *surrounded by agreeable companions,* when we *are at our ease.*

Thus, it at once becomes plain that the cranial and sacral divisions operate in direct opposition to the sympathetic division, as has been said, for the quiet and pleasurable emotions that have been mentioned are just the opposite of fear.

So far, in the consideration of emotion, only the reactions caused by the autonomic system have been mentioned.

However, every emotion, the emotion of fear as well as any other, contains reactions *caused directly by the central nervous system.* Thus, in anger, the fists are clenched, the limbs are stiffened, the jaws are set. In grief, the body is bent, the corners of the mouth droop. In pride, the chest is held high, the head erect.

The sensations accompanying all these attitudes are, of course, reflected in the brain, where the total pattern constitutes the emotion.

Individuals differ greatly in their constitutional tendencies toward experiencing the strong emotions, such as fear. Some experience fear on very slight stimulation. Others are only moved by the very greatest crises.

But, now, just *why* is a person overtaken by stage fright?

The first answer is that *he is overtaken by fear.*

But why does the fear come?

The next answer is that *he perceives an emergency.*

This means that *he perceives a situation which he doubts his ability to meet.*

On perceiving this situation, at once his central nervous system — the one with which he perceives the situation that constitutes the emergency — sends impulses into the sympathetic division of the autonomic nervous system, and the whole train of disturbing symptoms is let loose.

But, pushing the question further, *what is there to fear?*

The answer to this question is long, for there are many things to fear, especially since any activity in which stage fright is experienced is likely to be one of the most complex activities in which an individual can engage.

"Oh, I'm Afraid They Won't Applaud!"

In the first place, there is danger that *the great fundamental instinct of desire for approval may be thwarted.* We all desire to be well thought of by our fellows and associates. Whenever this instinct is in danger of being thwarted, we perceive an emergency, and at once we are afraid—we experience fear.

A singer wishes to have applause at the end of his song.

A speaker wishes to be complimented on his speech.

An actor wishes to have his characterization praised.

A dancer wishes to have his skill complimented.

An athlete wishes to secure renown by winning his event.

i"Mon Dieu! What Is ze Second Line of Zat Song?"

If there seems to be the least danger that these ends may not be secured, then fear, or stage fright, sets in.

Let us take, in detail, the case of a woman singer. In the first place, she wishes to be properly

and beautifully gowned. Then, she wishes
her make-up to be just right. She wishes to
walk and stand in an attractive manner.
She hopes she is physically attractive. Further, she wishes to render her song perfectly.
She hopes that her voice will be in good condition; that she will remember her notes;
that she will remember her words; that she
will start off on the right key; that there will
be no flatting of her high notes, no slurring.
She hopes that she and her accompanist will
keep together; that her pronunciation and
diction will be acceptable; that she has
chosen the right song to sing; that the audience will like it; that she will have real emotional fervor in her singing; that she will get
hearty applause; that she will be encored!
Thus, in a hundred little ways, her desire for
approval is in danger of being thwarted, and
so she is beset with fear.

Take also, the case of a male speaker. He, too,
wishes to be properly dressed. He hopes
his trouser legs are not too long nor too
short; that his tailor was up-to-date in the
cut of his coat and vest; that his tie is properly adjusted, and his collar of the proper
fashion; that his hair is properly cut and
properly combed. He wishes his voice to
be in good condition. He wishes his pronunciation to be correct and acceptable.

If he is going to speak extemporaneously, he hopes he will not get tangled up in his sentence structure; that he will remember the outline of his speech; that he will not make

BANQUET HALL

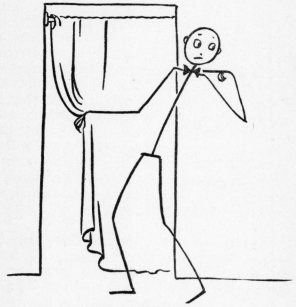

"How's My Tie, Bill?"

any mistakes in the facts that he is going to present; that his reasoning will be sound; that he will speak long enough and not too long. He hopes his movements will not be awkward; that his gestures will be effective;

that he may use facial expression to advantage. He hopes his mental attitudes will be proper, that he will be neither too modest nor too egotistic; that he will not hurt anybody's feelings.

If he is going to present an argument, he hopes he can win his audience to his point of view. If he is narrating something, he hopes his story will be interesting. If he is describing something, he hopes his description will be clear and pleasing. If he is explaining something, he hopes his audience will understand. If he is going to tell a humorous story, he hopes his audience will laugh. He hopes the audience will applaud with real enthusiasm when he has finished.

An actor wishes to be physically attractive; to have an excellent "stage presence." He hopes his costume is authentic and effective. He is anxious about every least detail of his make-up. He hopes that he can remember his lines; that his voice will be clear and strong. He hopes he may emphasize the proper words, giving each exactly the right quality, force, and pitch. He hopes that his rate of utterance and his pauses will be just right; that his fellow actors will give him good support; that the curtain will go up and come down at the proper times; that nothing will go wrong with the lighting effects; that the critics will treat him kindly; that he can please the director.

If he is playing comedy, he hopes he will amuse the audience and keep them laughing. If he is playing tragedy, he hopes he can inspire pity and fear, and wring the hearts of his hearers. On every occasion, he hopes his audience will tell their friends that it was a good "show," and that the play will have a good run.

So, whether the performer be a singer, or a speaker, or an actor, there is always plenty to worry about, and it is small wonder that he is beset with fear.

Moreover, each individual performer has specific and personal shortcomings that are constantly to be guarded against, and these, especially, make him anxious and fearful.

But the fear that besets a singer, a speaker, or an actor is not always confined to matters that concern the immediate audience. There

"Say Tom, Do You Say 'The Committee IS' or 'The Committee ARE'?"

are always outside matters that are fraught with possibilities of success or defeat. Other instincts, besides that of desire for approval, are involved.

First, there may be mentioned the desire for
financial gain. The singer wishes a better
contract, increased remuneration. The
speaker may know that whether he receives

A Financial Emergency May Cause Stage Fright.

a promotion in his firm will depend upon the
success of his speech. The actor may know
that a better part and increased salary will
be the outcome of success in his present part.
This particular concert, this particular

speech, this particular characterization in a play, may be the means of opening a life-long career of success or of closing forever the door of opportunity.

"What If He Does That to Me!"

Another instinct whose thwarting may result in an emergency and consequently give rise to fear in a speaker, singer, or actor is the instinct of rivalry. Perhaps there is no world so shot through with rivalry as the world of the artist. Last week Madame Soprano sang in this very city, in this very hall, before these same people; tonight the singer must outdo her. Last month Senator Spellbinder spoke to the Democrats before this same club and was highly praised; today, his arguments must be answered and his case demolished. Renowned Matinee Idol has just closed a most successful run in his new play; this opening night must make his acting seem amateurish. So, the singer, speaker, or actor, perceives an emergency, and is upset.

Parental affection, even, may depend for its satisfaction upon the outcome of tonight's performance. The kiddies must have schooling. They must be given dancing lessons. And whether the performer will be able to give them these advantages will depend on tonight's success or failure.

There may be, too, a lover or sweetheart in the audience, or waiting for the morning paper, who must, at all hazards, be favorably impressed.

Thus, factors that will give rise to fear may exist far outside the immediate situation in which the artist finds himself.

Sometimes, in the case of an individual who is inexperienced, and has never before faced a similar situation, simply the fear of the unknown causes stage fright. Even with

experienced performers, when a new and
unique situation is encountered, the same
fear of the unknown sets in. The great actor,
Joseph Jefferson. although he had faced thou-
sands of audiences on the stage, experienced
a bad case of stage fright
when he attempted to make
a speech before a university
audience. Many a preacher,
used to speaking to docile
congregations, will visibly
tremble in the presence of
a howling university pep-
meeting crowd.

Perhaps Your Stage Fright Dates Back to a Childhood Experience

Some people seem to be overcome with fear upon
appearing before even a small group, and
when nothing extremely important seems to
be at stake. Such people can usually trace

their fear to childhood or former experiences when they were laughed at. If, as a child, you stubbed your toe and went sprawling on the sidewalk and were laughed at, you are likely to experience qualms of fear in almost any situation where there is danger of making a false step. If, in school, in making a recitation, you mispronounced a word and your schoolmates snickered, you are likely still to be sensitive whenever you use language before a group.

Psychiatrists say that many performers suffer stage fright because as children they were criticized by their elders. They were told that they should be seen, not heard, and as a result a fear of letting themselves go has persisted into adulthood.

Sometimes people who are not at all afraid will tremble in a situation which results in great stimulation. A great hall, filled with people, with a band playing loud music, in the midst of gay and colorful decorations, will often cause members of the crowd to tremble. A little girl who had never played the piano before a large audience, but who was perfectly confident of her ability, said, after her performance: "My foot trembled on the pedal, Daddy! What made that?" Here was a case where no fear in the ordinary sense seems to have been present, and the symptoms surprised even the artist! Some such thing as mere overstimulation seems to have caused the disturbance.

Still another reason for stage fright is sometimes advanced. According to this theory, there is a conflict between instincts. As one author has put it, "One-half of the man wants to

Sometimes Stage Fright Is Simply Due to Overstimulation

run away, and the other half wants to stay and give the speech." This conflict causes opposing impulses in the nervous system which manifest themselves in trembling (the conflict between the abductor muscles and the adductor muscles), in absurd word combinations, and, on the whole, in great and intense effort that results in no action and no utterance.

Sometimes it is said that a speaker, singer, or actor "freezes," that is, becomes perfectly

Just a Case of Frozen Eloquence!

still — cannot move and cannot speak. This reaction is traced back to the primitive days of man, when, like a rabbit today, he became extremely still in the presence of danger, hoping thus to avoid drawing attention to himself.

TREATMENT III
THE REMEDIES FOR STAGE FRIGHT

Now that the causes of stage fright have been set forth, the various ways of relieving it can be more easily prescribed.

First, it should be remembered that stage fright is *an emotional upset, due to the presence of an emergency.*

Therefore, the first thing to do is to *minimize the emergency,* that is, make it seem smaller and less important.

And here we enter upon a long train of remedies, for, just as the emergency may arise for many different reasons, so there must be many different means of cure.

As has been pointed out, probably the risk that the instinct for approval may be thwarted is the first great cause of stage fright. But this general risk is usually made up of several specific and smaller risks.

First, let us take up the case of the woman singer. It was said in the chapter dealing with the causes of stage fright that the woman singer, among other things, desires to be properly and beautifully gowned. If there is the least suspicion in her own mind that she may not be, this fact will play its own little part in bringing on an attack of stage fright. Therefore, she should be careful to see that this contributing cause is re-

An Artist Should Employ the Best Modistes and Read the Best Fashion Magazines

moved. How may she do it? First of all anyone who wishes to be a public singer should, from her early youth, be a student of the very best fashion magazines. She should be observant of the best dressed women. She should, as much as possible, buy her clothes at the most stylish shops or employ the very best *modistes*. She should go to many concerts and observe how the

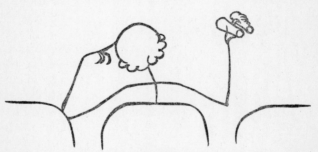

A Young Singer Should Carefully Observe the Dress of the Best Artists on the Concert Platform

artists dress. She should, with the aid of her dressmakers, study her own personality and see that her clothes emphasize her good points and minimize her poor ones. In these, and many other ways, she should, through the years, build up a superlative judgment in the choice of clothes. Thus, when the occasion for a public appearance arrives, she will be perfectly at ease in regard to her clothes, at least, and this one cause of stage fright will have been removed.

I WONDER IF I'M STANDING ALL RIGHT

Solicitude as to Posture Sometimes Upsets an Artist

To be careless in the matter of clothes, to leave the choosing of the gown to the last minute, to wear last year's gown, is but to court a nervous disturbance on the evening of the performance. The time to be apprehensive in the matter of clothes is not the last day before the concert, nor the last week, nor the last month, but *constantly through the years*. Only when good taste and judgment have been developed over a long period of time can there come an absolute forgetting of the matter of proper gowning on any particular occasion.

And there is another matter closely associated
with the choice of the gown, namely, the
ability to wear it gracefully. This ability,
like the ability to choose the gown, can only
be developed over a period of time. If you
have ever seen a raw girl from the country,
or the village hoyden, attend her first dance
in an evening gown, you will know what is
meant.

Now, as to make-up: Here, too, good taste and
judgment must be built up over a period of
time. It will not do to be careless day after
day, and night after night, and then suddenly become solicitous the day of the performance. A woman may trust her make-up
to the very best beauticians, but if she is not
accustomed to being made up in the particular way that the beautician has chosen, she
is bound to have the matter on her mind, to
have a faint wondering as to her coiffure,
her rouge, her lipstick, her eyebrow pencil,
and thus to be somewhat disturbed.

How conscious of gait some artists seem to be
as they walk over to the piano or come to
the front of the stage! Why? Because they
have not practiced the technique of walking
under such circumstances. Teachers of singing are often at fault here. Working day
after day with the voice and notes, they are
prone to leave all other matters to the artist
herself. They say they cannot be respon-

sible for all the hundred and one things that enter into the personalities of their students. But there is more to concert singing than the ability to strike a high *A* on the musical scale, or execute a trill, or secure good quality, or come successfully through a complicated phrase. Such matters as stage presence, a good gait, and graceful movements also contribute to the general success, and should not be neglected. Therefore, the prospective artist should seek out those teachers who attend to these matters, should daily practice walking on

Practice This! It May Help Your Stage Fright Some Day!

and off the stage, should cultivate grace in movement. Thus, [one more contributing cause of stage fright will be removed.

Some people are prone to believe that as God made them so are they doomed to remain all their lives. Nonsense! To be physically

attractive is not altogether a matter of inheritance. It is also a matter of cultivation.
A physically attractive person, nine chances
out of ten, given a fairly good inheritance,
has developed attractiveness through proper
physical training. To be sure, this does not
mean that there has been a course in physical training, but in *some* way there has been
physical development. If then a woman
singer desires to be physically attractive, she
should, all her days, be busy in those ways
that will give her that womanly beauty that
is so winning on the concert platform.

But a singer should be able to sing! This means
a long and arduous course of training. And
with the best teachers! To try to economize
by securing a cheap teacher is to throw the
future into the discard. Bad habits may thus
be developed that will ruin a voice for life.
The formative years are the most precious
years. They are the years in which change
and development are at their zenith. As the
months and years go by, inevitably harden-
ing processes set in, and it becomes more
and more difficult to change habits. Therefore, from the very first lesson to the very
last consultation with the expert, there
should be constant companionship with those
who really know. Then, when the artist
stands on the platform, she will *know that
she is right!* Her training will have put her

at her ease vocally. She will not be nervous
because she is not quite sure as to the correctness of her method or execution.

Keep to the Right, Young Lady!

And here a word of caution should be inserted
about trying to "arrive" too quickly. Many
a bad case of stage fright has been experienced because the artist has attempted too

much too early. The master portrait painter puts in the highlight in the eye with what seems to be the grossest carelessness. But what is mistaken for carelessness is but the superlative co-ordination of his muscles that has been developed through the painting of a thousand portraits and the putting in of two thousand highlights. So it is with the singer. She must have sung a thousand songs before that masterful touch may come which always bespeaks the true artist. Thus, to attempt an engagement beyond one's powers is to beget an anxiety as to outcome that may well constitute an emergency and, therefore, cause stage fright.

And memory! Will the notes be remembered? Will the words be remembered? Here often a very real emergency is met, one that causes no end of stage fright. The singer must be absolutely certain of her memory, else she courts serious nervous disturbance.

How may one be sure in regard to matters of memory? The answer lies in the laws that govern this particular function of the mind.

To begin with, the *ability to remember anything varies almost directly with the number of repetitions*. This means, to the artist, that the words and tune must be repeated again and again. No hurried preparation, consisting of going over the song only a few times, will suffice. Day after day, month after month, must be devoted to getting the performance ready for presentation.

Second, the *vividness or intensity of the impression determines how well anything will be remembered.* This means that the artist must seek every means to make the tune and the words vivid in her experience. She may use colored inks, she may act out the song, she may have someone else sing what she is to render, she may write out the notes and the words, she may even print the whole song with a camel's hair brush on a giant sheet of bristol board! *Some way must be developed* to make the song *vivid.*

Third, if the singer is to remember the tune and words of her song or part, she *must develop her sense of rhythm, and synchronize the words and notes with this rhythm.* This is one place where the singer has a tremendous advantage over the speaker, for rhythm is one of the great essentials of all music. Part of her work is, therefore, done for her.

Fourth, *material to be remembered should be learned as a whole, rather than split up into parts which are separately learned.* The singer,

therefore, will not learn the tune staff by
staff, phrase by phrase, nor learn the words
line by line, but will learn the complete tune
and words as a whole. Thus, the mental
processes of association that are so important in all memory work will be furthered.
There will be no gaps where logical connection is not made, and once the performance
is begun, it will be run off as a unit.

Fifth, *if anything is to be read and remembered,
it should* be read as rapidly as possible. Here
again the logical connections are more ade-
quately preserved and the close approxima-
tion of the various parts in point of time aids
in the recall. So the song should be read
through rapidly, not dawdled over piece by
piece.

Sixth, *if something is to be learned, it is better to
intersperse the learning with periods of rest
rather than to keep repeating it over and
over again at one sitting.* Hence, long hours
of practice, without rest periods, should be
avoided. "Work a while, then rest," should
be the practice in preparing for a public performance. And the periods of rest should
be at least ten minutes in length, preferably
more.

Seventh, *each period of committing to memory
should be followed by a period of mental quiet,
rather than by a period of activity devoted to*

something else. To switch from one task directly to another is bad policy, for the

*Periods of Practice Should be Interspersed
with Periods of Rest*

second task is likely to obliterate the effect of the first. Yet if the two tasks are widely dissimilar, the effect of obliteration is less. To abandon the practice of one song, therefore, and immediately begin practicing

another is the height of folly. The artist
who desires to remember on the platform
should practice and then rest, or turn to
some activity of an entirely different nature.

*To Go on a Party Just before a Performance Is To Court
a Bad Case of Stage Fright*

Eighth, *the more recently something to be remembered is gone over, the greater the chance of its
being remembered.* For an artist, therefore,
to go to a week-end party the last two or

three days before a concert would be to endanger success. No experienced artist would ever indulge in such foolishness, of course, but the inexperienced, caught by the drive for amusement that is so strong in youth, might very well yield to the temptation.

That's Right, Little Girl, Understand It!

Ninth, *if anything is to be remembered, it should be understood.* Nonsense is the most difficult thing on earth to remember! To attempt to sing a song in a foreign language when the words are not understood, is to court failure at the outset. The singer should sit down quietly and puzzle out the meaning, or, better, study it out intelligently. If a year or two of study of the foreign language is the price of understanding the song, then it should be paid.

How often a singer is disturbed and becomes nervous because she and the accompanist do not keep together! How often one or the other is just a little bit ahead! Doubtless there is an art of accompanying. It may be possible that when both the singer and the accompanist are real artists, a song may be executed by them without rehearsal. But to omit frequent and thorough rehearsals is to tempt Fate. No matters of expediency or diplomacy should ever be allowed to interfere with the choice of an accompanist or with frequent rehearsals. It is much better for an artist simply to refuse to sing than to attempt to sing when not sure of that superb co-ordination between accompanist and artist that marks the artistic performance.

Then, if the singer is to avoid another source of nervousness, she should look to her pronunciation, her diction. This is usually taught along with singing, but a thorough grounding in general phonetics will be found of great advantage. Knowing the different sounds that are given to the letter *r* in various languages, for instance, or the different ways in which a *k* can be uttered, she will feel much more sure of herself, and will not doubt her ability as to pronunciation and diction, thus avoiding nervousness at the outset.

"Will they like this song?" is a question that may arise in the mind of the singer and cause her to be nervous. The cure for stage fright from this cause lies in a long practical study of programs and audiences. As many concerts as possible should be attended and close observation made as to the effects of different kinds of songs. A popular audience will like a simple song, full of "heart interest." An audience highly educated in music will like a complicated musical pattern and a score that demands the highest technique. But nothing will banish fear as to the choice of a song but close study of audience effects and long practical experience.

Such a catalog of matters that may throw a woman singer into a case of stage fright is, of course, not exhaustive. However, it shows that one of the best ways to overcome fear is to be master of the situation, to have no doubt as to one's ability.

Now let us take the case of a male speaker. He also may be upset, and experience stage fright, because he is not quite certain as to

the correctness of his dress, his voice, his
pronunciation.

"Don't try to economize on clothes!" is a good
motto for a man who speaks much in public.
To wear a suit made by the best tailor in
town is to give one's nerves a great sedative.
Such clothes always feel better and look
better. One feels that he can face any audience and not be ashamed.

As to voice, it is necessary, if courses in voice
training have been neglected in school or
college, to take a course in voice culture from
some good professional teacher. The Extension Divisions of Universities usually offer
such courses and they will be found of great
benefit. If there is no University Extension
class in voice culture at hand, often the
teacher of public speaking in the local high
school offers evening classes where much can
be learned. Private lessons with a good
teacher are well worth their price.

Too much cannot be said in the way of advising
business men who speak to keep in good
physical condition. When a man is in good
health and rested, his voice has a ring and
a vibrancy that cannot be secured by the
man who is slightly ill all the time or who
has "been out on a party" the night before.
If a business man has not the time to get

himself into good physical condition before a speech, he should refuse the invitation to speak. Otherwise his anxiety as to the condition of his voice may throw him into a panic.

If Your're Ashamed of Your Voice, Try this a Few Times Each Week!

As to pronunciation, the American public is extremely tolerant. It will overlook mispronunciations and those pronunciations that are provincial or dialectic, provided the speaker's message is sane and forceful, or is humorous, or has other good qualities. However, any speaker will be more acceptable if he really knows his English. And there is no short cut to efficiency in the use of language. It comes only through years of study and constant alertness as to the use of words. Any man who feels that in his school or college days his language training was neglected should, therefore, devote his spare time and evenings to linguistic studies. He will thus, over a period of time, come to feel confident in his use of English and not feel fear on that score when he faces his audience.

A good, thorough course in grammar is one of the best cures for stage fright when a speaker feels nervous concerning his sentence structure. It is to be regretted that formal grammar was for many years neglected in the schools. It furnishes a superb check on one's use of language. And here again, if good training in grammar has not been secured in school or college, a good substitute is found in the Extension classes offered by high schools and universities. There are, also, a number of good correspondence courses offered by commercial publishers and by various educational institutions.

What has been said in regard to remembering
the notes and words of a song applies equally

Prepare in Advance to Conquer Your Stage Fright

well to the remembering of a speech. Just
to save time in turning back to them the
nine laws of memory are here presented

briefly in tabular form as they apply to a speech:

1. A speech should be rehearsed as many times as possible.

2. Various ways should be devised to make the speech vivid in the speaker's mind.

3. If the speech can in some way be made to possess rhythm, either as to outline or phraseology, there will be greater chance that it will be easily remembered.

4. The speech, either in outline or in fully developed form, should be learned as a whole rather than in parts.

5. If a speech is to be committed to memory, it should be read over and over again as rapidly as possible.

6. All periods devoted to learning a speech should be interspersed with intervals of rest. These periods should be at least ten minutes long.

7. A period devoted to learning a speech should be followed by one of mental quiet. To turn immediately to some other mental task is to obliterate much of what has just been learned.

8. The speech should always be gone over, at least mentally, just before it is given. To speak the speech aloud, if it is not so long as to tire the voice, is best.

9. No speaker should ever attempt to say anything that he doesn't understand.

When a speaker is not sure of his facts, he is quite likely to be overtaken by stage fright. He must know that what he says is true. He must have observed his facts himself, and not be in error in regard to his observation, or he must have gleaned his facts from the very best authorities.

To Be Sure of Your Facts Is One Way To Cure Your Stage Fright

To make a correct personal observation, that is, to be sure that one has really seen what he thinks he has seen, is a very difficult matter,

and there are several things about which
every speaker should be careful.

First, he should see to it that he is in good health.
Poor health warps observation. An individual so handicapped will find himself overlook-
ing things that he should see, being irritated
by things that he should view calmly, mis-
understanding the words and moods of what
he hears. He may be careless of detail.

Second, he should be sure that all his sense
organs are perfect, and functioning in a normal way. If an observer is color blind, or
is afflicted by astigmatism, or is near-sighted
or far-sighted, or is partially deaf, or has an
impaired sense of smell, his observations in
many fields will be entirely unreliable. A
man with a "hang-over" from a drinking
bout of the night before is not a very good
judge of the savoriness of a breakfast!

Third, a speaker who wishes to be confident as
to facts gained from personal observation
should make sure that his observation was
conducted under the best conditions. A
poorly lighted room, a noisy room, a room
too hot or too cold, may cause great errors
in observation.

Fourth, a speaker should possess skill and training in the field in which he makes his observations. An astronomer can see things
through a telescope that will utterly elude

the layman. Likewise the biologist can see things through a microscope that no ordinary person can make out. Knowledge brings the power to discriminate. The casual visitor to an engine room may be startled by seeing the engineer suddenly get up and turn some valve or pull some lever, at the same time making some remark about the efficiency of his engine. To the visitor no change in the sounds of the engine room has been apparent, but to the highly skilled engineer there has been a marked change. The ordinary automobile driver cannot with precision locate the knock or tap in his motor, but to the skilled mechanic its source is obvious.

Fifth, observation depends greatly upon attention. We do not observe well those things to which we pay no attention. A farmer crossing a field pays attention to the crop that is growing in it; an entomologist to the insects that infest it; a soil erosion expert to the shifts in the soil; an oil geologist to the contour of the landscape and the cropping out of certain kinds of rock; a painter to the various colors of the vegetation.

Sixth, the observation of a speaker is often faulty, since it tends to be warped by the value to him of the thing observed. It is an old proverb that we see those things we are looking for. A person standing in front of a

magazine rack, hunting for a certain periodi-
cal, can rarely tell afterwards what magazines were in the rack — he knows only that
the one he was looking for was not there.

Seventh, to be certain of one's facts one should be
sure of the accuracy of the instruments used
in the observations. Were the scales accurate, was the telephone in good working order,
was the thermometer a reliable one — such
questions should be constantly asked.

If a speaker, then, would avoid fear as to correctness of facts gleaned from personal observation, he should be careful that the preceding seven conditions were present when
he made his observations.

But, of course, we must take some facts on the
say and observations of others. We cannot sail down the Nile on Cleopatra's barge.
We cannot talk with Julius Caesar or George
Washington. That these people ever lived
we must accept on the testimony of others.
Moreover, we cannot be present at all places
at all times. We must take our facts about the
recent earthquake in Japan on the mere word
of someone who was there and experienced it.

Whom, then, should a speaker trust?

Here are some good questions to ask yourself
when you are about to quote someone else
in regard to facts:

1. Was the person quoted an accurate observer?

2. Did he have precise power of expression, that is, did he say exactly what he meant?

3. Did the person really make the statements attributed to him? Where? When? Before whom?

4. Was he capable of expert testimony?

5. Did he have opportunity to really observe the facts in regard to which he is quoted?

6. Was he prejudiced?

7. Do others agree with him?

8. Did he give all the facts?

*To Be Sure of Your Facts, and Thus Conquer Stage Fright,
You Shouldn't Believe All You Read!*

No one should believe all he reads. Because a thing is in print is no criterion of its truthfulness.

Therefore, every speaker should be careful as to the authorities whom he chooses to quote.

If a speaker, then, will be careful as to the facts that he himself has observed, and if he will be careful to choose dependable authorities when he wishes to quote others as to facts, he will find himself much more confident and will be much less liable to be overtaken by stage fright.

That a speaker must be certain that his reasoning is sound goes without saying. If he cannot trust himself in his thinking, there is good reason for any stage fright that he feels. To develop confidence in one's thinking is no easy task. It demands a great deal of study. Probably the best way to be sure that one thinks correctly is to buy some good text on argumentation and study it slowly and thoroughly. There are many such on the market and any bookseller can easily order one of them if he hasn't it in stock.

As for posture, movement, and gesture, there is no substitute for a good teacher. Again, classes in public speaking conducted by universities and high schools can be highly recommended.

As for general mental attitudes, it does but little good to try to assume an attitude on the platform that has not become a daily habit. Attitudes of friendliness, sympathy, and earnestness will aid any speaker, but let him not try to assume them merely for the few moments that he is before an audience. Rather, he should build them into his life. One cannot be a grouch all day, and then suddenly appear friendly on the platform at

Attending a University Extension Class in Public Speaking is a Good Way to Conquer Stage Fright

8 P.M. One cannot be lackadaisical week after week, and then seem to care a great deal about something when the time comes to make a speech. Personality and character

building is a matter of years. Let every
speaker, then, who would avoid stage fright
caused by anxiety as to proper mental attitudes devote all his waking hours to the
building up of an attractive personality in
all his dealings. Then, on the platform, he
can be simply himself, and experience no
fear as regards matters of mental attitude.

As for skill in description, narration, and exposi-
tion, there can be no substitute for a good
course in rhetoric. The study of a good
book on rhetoric will be found invaluable,
and a correspondence course, if it is not
possible to attend a university or high school
course, will be found of value.

*Thus, much of the whole matter of avoiding stage
fright in speaking can be reduced to the simple
words "develop confidence." When a speaker
is sure of himself in every regard he will find
his fear has largely disappeared. He will
have removed the cause of the emergency and he
will be in a state of comparative nervous calm.*

Perhaps one of the best examples of a man who
was a great speaker because of this confidence in himself was Senator Albert J. Beveridge, of Indiana. Says one of his classmates
at De Pauw University: "There he stands,
closing a debate, earnest, resolute, confident,

George Arliss

George Arliss as Nathan Rothschild
In *The House of Rothschild* (20th Century Picture)

yet alert, his whole soul thrown into his speech. Others might be languid in public speech, not Beveridge. Others might trifle, Beveridge never. As he approached his climax and his voice rose in staccato, vigorous, ringing tones, accompanied by flashing eye and animated action, the audience was more than carried completely before him." Another classmate says: "I have been on a debating team many times when Beveridge was on the other side. He was always prepared, treated his subject like an expert, and his confidence that he understood the subject gave him confidence in his debating. I remember how Beveridge, when called upon to speak, used to walk perfectly straight, manifesting power before he said a word. He was always at his best. He seemed to expect to win, acted like he was going to win, and he did win."

One concrete suggestion at this point will be found of great value. It is that a speaker should never attempt to speak, should never accept an invitation to speak, upon a topic that he does not feel himself qualified to discuss. So many clubs find difficulty in making up their programs that their committees are inclined to force speakers into situations where they cannot do themselves justice. Such program committees should be resisted. A speaker owes much to himself.

He should do only those things that he knows he can do well. Bricklayers should not discuss Rembrandt's portrait painting, nor plumbers the musical art of Chopin.

If You Wish to Avoid Stage Fright, Don't Talk on a Topic You Know Nothing About

Neither should musicians discuss the manufacture of medicinal chemicals, nor painters the training of race horses. "Let the shoemaker stick to his last."

What has already been said in regard to the singer and the speaker applies, with but very little change, to the actor. To avoid stage fright, the actor must be sure of himself in all the phases of his technique.

To begin with, he must be sure of his costume. It would be surprising to know what care the best actors devote to their costumes. They study the fashion plates of the period in which the play is supposed to occur, often spending hours in museums and among dusty volumes of extensive libraries. If the play is foreign, they study the magazines of the country in which the action takes place. They study the portraits by great artists, the caricatures of the great cartoonists. They buy books that present the country and its inhabitants pictorially. If possible, when the play is laid in their own countries, they visit the place where the scene is laid and study the characters with which the play deals. George Arliss, in preparation for his famous character Disraeli, visited a museum, noticed a particular waistcoat of the time of Disraeli which had an attractive lace trimming, and hired a young seamstress to copy it.

Then, the actor must be sure of his make-up. David Warfield once said: *"First,* look the part. *Then* act it."* Such actors as Paul Muni gain much of their composure because they know they *look* the part. The facial lines, the dress of the hair or wig, the veins in the hands, the exact complexion, all receive the most detailed care.

As for remembering the part, enough has already been said concerning the singer and speaker to suggest to the actor the best procedure. The fact that the actor often depends on the cues supplied him by his fellow actors need not be disconcerting, if the actor is willing to know his play thoroughly enough.

What has been said, also, concerning the voice of the singer and speaker applies with equal force to the actor. Only long and assiduous vocal training under the best of instructors can give confidence.

To develop confidence, then, is the first great remedy for stage fright, whether the performer be a singer, a speaker, or an actor.

It is often well, if stage fright persists even after all the precautions against it have been taken in the way of adequate preparation for the task in hand, to probe back into childhood experiences in order to see if there may not be some forgotten experience of self-consciousness at the root of the disturbance. If the experience from which the fear takes its origin can be uncovered, there is the

Photo by Elmer Fryer, Warner Bros. F. N. Studios

Paul Muni

Paul Muni as Zola in "The Life of Zola"
(A Warner Bros., F. N. Picture)

chance that its effect may be minimized. We rarely fear those things that we understand. Thus, if the singer, speaker, or actor can think himself back into his childhood and see the real reason why his associates laughed at him, and can see that the whole matter was trivial, he has gone a long way toward banishing his fear. Perhaps the experience dates from "speaking a piece" on Friday afternoon; perhaps from a spectacular sprawl on the ice when skating; perhaps from a mispronounced word in a recitation; perhaps from the laughter of an amused Aunt or Uncle when a puerile observation was made at the dinner table. One speaker in a college class could definitely trace his fear in regard to the pronunciation of words to a recitation he once made in the eighth grade of the grammar school, when, while glibly reciting his history lesson, he said: "The general was killed, but his corpse (corps) swept the field!"

If stage fright is due to conflicting instincts, as when one-half the speaker, singer, or actor wants to run away and the other half to stay, one remedy consists in deliberately breaking the deadlock by *doing something*, almost no matter what. Mental "drainage" must be started. Some one brain center must take control. Action, action of any sort, tends to start this mental drainage,

and after it is once started it may be
directed into the proper channel. Thus, a
speaker may take a drink of water, may turn

*In Some Cases of Stage Fright, One-half the Speaker
Wishes to Run Away and the Other Half
to Stay and Give the Speech*

over several pages of his notes, may stride
to another part of the platform. He may
indulge in an emphatic gesture — it makes

no difference whether there is anything to emphasize or not. Once the gesture is executed, new mental associations are set up and something, at least, more or less remotely connected with the topic of the speech, can be said.

This matter of conflict, however, does not always confine itself to such fundamental factors as the instincts. Sometimes the deadlock occurs where merely ideas are concerned. Thus, a speaker may have a multitude of ideas flood in upon him, and be unable to make a choice between them. The cure in this case is the same as in a conflict of instincts. Some definite decision must be made, something must be said or done. Henry Ward Beecher once found himself in such a predicament, and solved the difficulty by shouting in a loud voice the one word "Oh!" (And the papers the next morning complimented him upon the exclamation and the dramatic pause that accompanied it!) A college debater who became confused while giving his summary in a debate suddenly stopped, put his hand to his throat, called for a drink of water, drank it, and by that time had broken his mental deadlock and was able to proceed. A high school prize orator having lost his bearings because he had substituted a synonym for a certain word at the end of a sentence, put in the sentence "The thoughts struck off at the moment are the thoughts that rule the world." The sentence had no connection with what the speaker was saying, but it "kept up the flow," started the machinery going, and enabled the speaker to get back on the mental track. (And, much to the disparagement of the intelligence of the audience, no one seemed to notice the lack of logic in the paragraph!)

The well-known teacher of public speaking Dale Carnegie, in his book *Public Speaking*, suggests another expedient that may be used when a mental stoppage embarrasses a speaker. It is to make up a sentence concerning the idea contained in the last word of the previous sentence. This word has so recently passed the speaker's lips that he will have no trouble in remembering it. Thus, if a speaker has just closed a sentence with the word "alliance," he can say "Alliances, of course, may be merely commercial, or avowedly military." If still the next idea which he was to utter does not rise in his mind, he can further say "Military alliances always breed ill feeling," and so go on as far as is necessary to allow the intended idea to rise to the surface. This device is not recommended as one that will increase the speaker's reputation for being logical, but it affords a way to get things going when the whole thinking apparatus seems to have broken down.

One very effective, and incidentally thoroughly scientific, method of overcoming stage fright at the beginning of a speech is to indulge in some pleasantry, to smile, to tell a humorous story. The paying of graceful compliments, to the audience, to the preceding speaker or speakers, to the committee on arrangements, and so on, has long been one of the thoroughly acceptable ways of beginning a speech. The superficial explanation is that "it develops a good feeling between the speaker and the audience, it pleases the audience, it makes them feel that the speaker is human and is a 'good fellow'." But there is a more scientifically expressed way of saying the same thing that gives it more than empirical prestige. It has already been pointed out that the cranial and sacral divisions of the autonomic nervous system work in direct opposition to the sympathetic division. Hence, any activity in them tends to cut down the activity of the sympathetic division, which is responsible for the fear. Now, it has further been said that when the cranial and sacral divisions are active, we experience such emotions as we feel when we enjoy our work, when we are among agreeable companions, when we are at our ease. Therefore a smile, a graceful compliment, a humorous story, tends to produce just the sort of emotions that will lessen fear. This "pleasant beginning" device has been called "breaking the ice." It breaks through the cold, detached relation that, many times, indeed often, exists between an audience and an unknown speaker. It establishes an atmosphere of fellowship. By it, the speaker, on account of the friendly response of the audience, comes at once to feel at home, to be at ease, to enjoy his task, and to experience a friendly companionship with the audience.

Always Hide Behind Your Subject!

One of the great cures for stage fright, one that has come down through the years as a standard adjuration from the great teachers, is "hide behind your subject." If you are frightened, wish to get out of sight, have a tendency to "freeze," your subject offers you something to hide behind. It has already been pointed out that initial stage fright usually disappears as the artist warms to his work. This is accounted for by the fact that he no longer is devoting attention to any emergency that may be present, but is centered upon the work in hand. It is a well-known fact that two things cannot hold the center of attention at the same time. Hence when a speaker gives attention to developing the points of his speech, or when a singer devotes attention to executing the melody, or when an actor devotes attention to the rendition of the lines, the perception of any emergency *must* be pushed into a realm of less attention, and consequently there cannot longer be such great fear. "Get going on your task" is, then, one of the best ways to cause stage fright to subside.

This "shift of attention" theory for the overcoming of stage fright may be utilized in other ways. In one of the great universities the first assignment in the beginning courses is to explain something that can be held in the hands — a flower, a puzzle, a manufactured product. The mere handling of the exhibit seems to put the speaker at his ease. His attention is centered upon the exhibit, and cannot, therefore, be devoted to the perception of an emergency. Such a procedure, moreover, has a secondary psychological effect, namely, that since the audience begins at once to pay attention to the exhibit, the speaker feels that they are not paying attention to him and is therefore relieved.

For those brief moments when the speaker sits on the platform before beginning his speech, when a good case of stage fright can be developed, this same device of handling something will be found useful. To leaf through a book, to see that one's notes are in proper order, even gently to blow one's nose (?) will be found to relieve nervous tension. And at the speaker's desk, to push the light to one side, to move the water glass and pitcher (how the cartoonists like the water glass and pitcher!), gently to slide the vase of flowers this way or that, will be helpful. It relaxes the audience, too, and makes them feel that the speaker is somewhat at home, and a general feeling of ease is developed in the whole situation.

There is another phase to this "shift of attention" theory that is somewhat related to the "hide behind your subject" technique. It is called the "have a message" method. In this the speaker constantly keeps in mind the great purpose of his speech, the idea that he wishes to drive home. He constantly thinks of helping the audience in some way. He wishes to inform them, to wake them up to an evil, to inspire them to redoubled effort, or what not. Having his attention focused on this purpose, it cannot be devoted to the matter of fright.

"Don't be fearful of the mistakes you are going to make" is another good piece of advice to those who are affected by stage fright. We all make mistakes, and a hundred years from now, as the old saying goes, who will know the difference! Besides, most mistakes are merely trivial. One of the best speeches ever given before a certain Grocers' Association was made by a grocer of foreign birth who was awkward, poorly dressed, and who not only murdered, but frightfully mangled the King's English! But he made a good speech, had a good message, was in earnest about it, and was heartily applauded.

"Don't apologize" is a favorite with those who train speakers. It is not given solely to protect the speaker from an adverse judgment on the part of the audience, but also for its effect on the speaker himself. If the speaker constantly is prone to focus his attention on his shortcomings, the emergency is magnified. Listen to what Lawrence Tibbett says of his

experience in grand opera. "At first I seemed
to upset everybody's disposition, and most
of the time I was apologizing for some out-
landish error that held up the rehearsal.
Other members of the cast were making mistakes, but they laughed them off and nobody seemed to complain. After three of
the five weeks of rehearsal were past, I dis-
covered a great truth about human nature.
If you admit your weakness, if you con-
tinually apologize, people instinctively scold
you—whether it is at a Metropolitan rehearsal or at a contract bridge table. If you never
confess your sense of inferiority, if you airily
wave aside your errors as if they amounted
to nothing, people sneer at you not at all.
Therefore, I stopped apologizing. Instead
of moaning at a stupid error, I merely grinned
and shrugged my shoulders. No longer did
the stars bark at me!"

"Analyze the situation" is another good piece
of advice when fear is about to rise. Can
you speak to *one* person without feeling fear?
Of course you can! Can you speak to *five*?
Again the answer must be yes! Can you
speak to *ten*? What difference is there between these situations? And if the audience is composed of a *hundred* or a *thousand*,
what difference is there? Really, there is
nothing to be scared about in addressing
simply *numbers* of people. If you can talk

to the most intelligent man in your audience when he is alone, you can talk to an audience made up of any number like him!

Walter B. Pitkin, in his book *Take It Easy*, says something quite pertinent to this matter of analyzing the situation. Says he: "Some of our most upsetting tensions are caused by fear; and the most devastating fears are fears of the unknown. To be aware of a peril but not to understand it throws the human body into a supreme tension and panic. The very instant you know what the menace is, you begin to ease up. This points to a simple rule. Whenever you find yourself worrying, fearful, or tense, stop short and ask yourself: 'Well, just what am I worrying about? Of what am I afraid?' Then your troubles will be half over. For the very act of seeking the answer will of itself reduce your tensions."

The opposite of fear, of course, is confidence, that is, a belief in oneself. All an artist can do, therefore, to bolster up his belief in himself will be useful in overcoming stage fright. It is said that when one is blue with melancholy, one of the best cures is to sit down and write out a list of all past successes and blessings and a list of all the pleasant factors in the present situation. A speaker, or a singer, or an actor may use the same technique by listing in his mind all the reasons why he is worthy. One's strength, one's ability in a given situation, is greatly aided by such a process. "You can," goes an old adage, "because you think you can." One of the leading neurologists of England reports an experiment carried on with three soldiers of the British army. "I asked the three men," says he, "to submit themselves to a test designed to measure the effect of their mental attitude on their physical strength, this strength to be measured by a single gripping device operated by the right hand. In their normal state these three men had an average grip of 101 pounds. When under hypnosis I told them they were weak, their utmost effort registered only 29 pounds. But when, still keeping them under hypnosis, I told them they were very strong, their average strength jumped back to the normal 101 pounds and then rose to 142 pounds. They were actually 40% stronger when they believed they were strong, and actually 70% weaker when they believed they were weak."

In the case of speakers, a word may be said about methods of preparation and delivery. Although there are some situations where the circumstances demand it, on the whole it is better not to commit a speech to memory. It is better to use the extemporaneous method. But what is technically called the extemporaneous method should be carefully distinguished from the impromptu method. In the impromptu method, the individual essays to speak without any preparation whatsoever. He simply gets up and talks. Very little good speaking results from this method, and unless the speaker is a mere "gabble-mouth," he is likely to run into plenty of difficulties that will throw him into a spasm of stage fright. But in the extemporaneous method the speaker makes a careful outline beforehand and then follows the outline while he is speaking, making up his sentences as he goes along. The extemporaneous method is likely to result in less stage fright than the committed speech because the mind is kept more active upon the matter of the speech and consequently cannot dwell on extraneous matters, such as dress, voice, gesture, the condition of the audience, and so on. After a speech is committed to memory, it often runs itself off with but little conscious attention on the part of the speaker. This can never be the case with the extemporaneous speaker. His attention is kept off the mechanics of delivery, and consequently worry concerning them never arises.

Much of what has just been said, it will be seen, has to do with what is often called auto-suggestion. In auto-suggestion one talks to himself, constantly suggesting to himself things that should be kept in mind. This process will be found of value in keeping the attention off the emergency. A speaker can say to himself "There is nothing to be afraid of. I know more about this topic than anybody out front. These people will be glad to hear what I have to say." And so on. Soon, under this treatment, he will find his fear symptoms vanishing.

Thus far, the remedies that have been suggested for stage fright have concerned the mental or psychological factors involved.

However, there are also many physical expedients that may be resorted to in an effort to eliminate the symptoms.

Probably the greatest and most effective of these is slow, deep, and regular breathing. To revert to something that was said earlier, the performer should always remember that stage fright may be traced to the perception of an emergency, and that in man's primitive days usually this emergency was physical. Hence the first symptom that was likely to develop was a more rapid breathing. The diaphragm and rib muscles began to work more rapidly in order to supply enough oxygen to carry off the waste products caused by physical exertion. From the action of the breathing muscles, of course, there ensued a more rapid beating of the heart, sweating, and all the other symptoms. If, then, a preformer can get control of his diaphragm and breathing muscles there is a chance that all the other symptoms will be lessened. Such action is entirely possible since the breathing apparatus is controlled by both involuntary and voluntary muscles. In sleep, and most waking hours, the involuntary muscles are active, while the voluntary ones are at rest. But at any time an individual may "throw out of gear" the involuntary muscles and take a breath of his own will. Now in fright, of course, the involuntary muscles, under stimulation of the sympathetic division of the autonomic nervous system, are stimulated into marked activity. But, if these muscles are "thrown out of gear" and the deep, slow, and regular breathing indulged in by a purely voluntary process, nervous associations are set up which result in a lessening of the other symptoms. It is much as if the sympathetic division of the autonomic system said to itself, "There can't be much wrong, or the diaphragm wouldn't be slowing down and acting as if nothing were the matter. I guess things must be going fairly well. There is no need to keep issuing these other orders to cope with an emergency." And, thus, the whole reaction of the individual tends to return to a normal condition.

Another good piece of counsel is "Go slow!"
Here again the breathing apparatus is involved. Many a time, under the nervous
excitement of speaking, the diaphragm does
not come far enough up to reach a position
of rest. It starts back down too quickly.
Thus, the supply of oxygen, on account of
the shallow breathing, becomes cumulatively
less and less, until the speaker is "out of
breath." If with each breath the diaphragm
is allowed to come completely up and then
is forced completely down by the process of
taking a deep breath, the amount of oxygen
will be kept more nearly normal and there
will be no feeling of being "out of breath."
This going slowly, too, which the process of
breathing deeply involves, is just what an
audience enjoys at the beginning of a speech.
At the start of any speech the minds of the
audience are engaged in thinking of a hundred different things. Going slowly enables
the audience to "collect its thoughts," to
focus on what the speaker is saying.

Really, this matter of breathing deeply and
slowly is but a phase of a much larger technique that may be employed by a speaker,
namely, relaxation. A well-known textbook
(Woolbert's *Fundamentals of Speech*) has the
following to say: "Relax whatever muscles
are not needed to accomplish the thing you
are trying to do. Call on the legs for enough

energy to stand with, and no more; those muscles which by their opposition cause the trembling at the knees must be relaxed; the legs must be content to stand, not run. Reduce the extra muscular tension in the back and hips; so also the tension of the arms, hands, and especially the neck and face."

Here is another device that a stage-frightened individual may employ: *Put on a bold front.* Control the symptoms of fear. Assume an attitude of ease, even though you are not at ease. It is surprising how many of the symptoms of fear are not seen by the audience. Therefore, if you control the larger aspects of the symptoms, you probably are succeeding much beyond your expectations. Moreover, the attitudes of strength and ease really cause you to possess these virtues. The well-known James-Lange theory of the emotions is in point here — if we assume the reactions of an emotion, we are likely to feel that emotion, for the emotion is, in essence, simply the symptoms. Shakespeare was right when he said, in another connection, "Assume a virtue if you have it not." A captain in the United States Army once said: "We ask our men to stand erect not only because they present a better appearance when they stand erect, but also because, when they stand erect, they actually are more courageous and make better soldiers."

Assume an air of confidence, therefore, even if
you do not feel confident. Be an actor, if
need be — at least to the extent of control-
ling the outward manifestations of fear.
Most business men have had to put on a
"front" at times. Nearly everyone has felt
the necessity, at one time or another, of
assuming a semblance of composure, the
spirit of which he sadly lacked. "Whistling
to keep up our courage" is not an idle phrase;
it is psychologically accurate. As boys,
whistling and swaggering while walking down
a dark, fearsome street, gave us courage;
whereas if we once gave up to fear and
started to glance furtively around at weird
shadows, or to quicken our pace, the end was
usually an ignominious skurry for the door-
way of home. Likewise the chip on our
shoulder was a direct provocation to our
own pugnacious spirit. Therefore, assume a
show of boldness; control, with an iron hand,
any tendency to nervous exhibitions. Appear to be master of the situation, and it
will help you really to be master.

As a final prescription for mastering stage fright,
it should be pointed out that, unless it becomes too great, stage fright is really of
value. If one really comes to understand
the values of the fear that he experiences
on confronting an audience, he looks upon
its symptoms as symptoms of a condition

that will aid him, rather than hinder him in attaining success.

Ernesto Brúmen has said: "If a person does not experience a touch of nervousness or excitation before appearing in public, it is safe to assume that he is of a cold or phlegmatic nature, and such a person is totally unfitted for an artistic career. You see, it's the artist in us that makes us that way."

Bobby Jones testifies as follows: "I used to think that if I could suppress my feeling of nervousness when starting out to play a match, I could then play a better and more thoughtful game. I have since come to think that the man who goes placidly on his way is often the easiest fellow to beat, for it is only the high-strung temperament that rises above its own ability to meet a great occasion."

Professors Lockwood and Thorpe, in their book *Public Speaking Today*, say: "Nearly all good speakers will tell you that a certain degree of nervous excitement is necessary. If one is to do his best, the brain must be keyed up to concert pitch. A violent pulse and a sick fear at heart are usually only signs that one's whole being is alert to the task in hand."

M. Bautain once said: "Woe to him who experiences no fear before speaking in public! It shows him to be unconscious of the function which he is about to discharge, that he does not understand what truth is, whose apostle he himself should be, or that he little cares, and that he is not animated by that sacred fire that comes down from Heaven to burn the soul!"

Professor Richard D. T. Hollister, Professor of Public Speaking at the University of Michigan, in his book *Speech Making*, has this to say about the value of fear: "Nervousness is not a thing to be despised, but a thing to be mastered. It is that quickening power that lifts a true man out of the commonplace and makes him eloquent. When controlled, it makes the heart beat stronger, the blood flow steadier, and the mind work at higher efficiency."

Therefore, learn to distinguish between that overpowering fright that may cause you to fail and that stimulating nerve tension that will enable you to do your best. Say to yourself: "This disturbance I feel is not stage fright. It is merely a *wholesome anticipatory solicitude!*"